Also edited by Bill Bondurant

Offensive Football   1972

DEFENSIVE FOOTBALL

DEFENSIVE

EDITED BY BILL BONDURANT

NEW YORK 1974 ATHENEUM

FOOTBALL

Dick Anderson

AND

Nick Buoniconti

Photographs by Henry Fichner
Copyright © Dick Anderson, Nick Buoniconti
and Bill Bondurant
All Rights Reserved
Library of Congress catalog card number 73-80752
ISBN 0-689-10573-8
Published simultaneously in Canada by McClelland
and Stewart Ltd.
Composition by Connecticut Printers, Inc.,
    Hartford, Connecticut
Printed and bound by Halliday Lithograph Corporation,
    Hanover, Massachusetts
Designed by Kathleen Carey
First Printing September 1973
Second Printing August 1974

Contents

DEFENSIVE FOOTBALL

Introduction

FOR NICK BUONICONTI, it all started on a wet fall afternoon in Springfield, Massachusetts. He was nine years old, a fifth grader. This was going to be his first day of organized football. In borrowed shoulderpads and jersey, Nick told his mother he was going to try out for a neighborhood team.

He never got there, at least not that year. He slipped on the slick pavement while crossing the street to the park and broke his arm. So much for football as a nine-year-old.

But you can't keep a good middle linebacker down. Nick was back the next year—short, chubby, not very menacing looking. The coach told him he looked like a guard candidate.

"I want to play middle linebacker," Buoniconti said. So did some other players. A test was devised. Each candidate was asked to make six tackles on different runners.

"I got five out of six," Nick said. "I was the middle linebacker."

Twenty-two years later he still is, only now he's the middle linebacker on the world champions of professional football, the Miami Dolphins.

"A champion," Buoniconti says. "That is the highlight of a professional's career. It was the highlight of mine. In 1973, I finally made it. I was thirty-two years old."

It wasn't for lack of trying that Nick didn't make it sooner. As a high school player in Springfield, he made All-Western Massachusetts as linebacker as a freshman, sophomore, and senior. He sat out his junior year with a knee injury.

More than forty colleges offered him football scholarships. He chose Notre Dame. After a year under Coach Terry Brennan and three more under Joe Kuharich, Buoniconti emerged as an All-America linebacker, short and small for professional football. He was 5' 11" and weighed 210 pounds.

The Boston Patriots of the old AFL drafted him in the 13th round, which is to say they gave him one chance in 50 of making the club. Buoniconti

4

stuck. Lucky for the Patriots.

In seven years with Boston (now New England) Buoniconti was All-AFL five times. He made a reputation for himself as a fierce and wide-ranging tackler, a free-lance artist who would blitz at the drop of a quarterback's confidence. Then he was hurt, and Boston gave up on Nick Buoniconti.

The Patriots shipped him to the then-bedraggled Miami Dolphins in exchange for a linebacker named John Bramlett and a quarterback who had never played, Kim Hammond.

"What a steal," crowed Joe Thomas, then the Dolphins' personnel director. "That was my greatest trade. The greatest deal of my life."

Who is to dispute him? Both Hammond and Bramlett are long gone from the Patriots. But Buoniconti was an immediate smash in Miami. In 1969 under George Wilson, he was named All-AFL for the sixth time and the Dolphins named the reject linebacker their most valuable player.

Then came Don Shula, and the Dolphins were on their way. But for Buoniconti, it was a time of readjustment and learning. Under Wilson and with the Patriots, he had been allowed every freedom. He could blitz when he pleased, roam where he wanted. The field was his. Under Shula, it was different. Shula's defense demands strict discipline.

The zone allowed few freedoms. Buoniconti re-tooled his style and emerged as the leader of the new Dolphin defense. The Dolphins themselves knew who was valuable. Buoniconti immediately was named the best defensive back, a grouping that included linebackers.

In the Miami-Dallas 1972 Super Bowl, Dallas had a game plan. The plan: Get to Buoniconti, keep him out of the play, and we can beat the Dolphins. Dallas conceived special blocking pat-terns designed to cut off Nick. They worked, but Dallas had help. Nick took such a terrific jolt in the second period that he played the rest of the game in a fog. He played on instinct.

But 1973 was different. Buoniconti and the Dol-phin defense destroyed Washington in Miami's 14–7 Super Bowl triumph. In truth, the Dolphins hung up a shutout. Washington's lone touchdown came late in the fourth quarter on a blocked field goal.

Afterwards, in the dressing room, Buoniconti savored the ultimate triumph—a world champion-ship and an undefeated season. He was the field boss of Miami's now-famous "No-Name Defense."

"Now," he said, "maybe they'll recognize the things we've done." The Dolphins had the NFL's best defense in 1972; they led the league in giving up the fewest points and in yards rushing. Everywhere it counted, the Dolphin defense led.

And Buoniconti, an attorney in the off-season, wanted the No-Name Defense to be recognized.

"What does it take for people to say we're great?" he asked. "If we did this in New York City, all the murders would be on page two."

"Buoniconti gives us our experience," Coach Don Shula said. "He worked harder at being a middle linebacker in 1972 than he ever has in his life. He really studied it. And he did an outstanding job of leadership."

At thirty-two, Buoniconti isn't about to retire.

"This year," he says happily, "is my twelfth as a pro. Heck no, I'm not going to quit. I want to win it all again...."

For Dick Anderson, it started in a Colorado junior league. He was ten. The league supplied only half a uniform—shoulderpads, jersey, and helmet. The players wore blue jeans and sneakers. Most of them were older than Dick Anderson— one year, two years, three years.

The game, of course, was tackle football.

"To make it," he recalled, "I had to be a little

tougher. The kids I played against were bigger and stronger. If I wanted to compete, I had to hit hard."

He still does. As the All-NFL strong safety of the Miami Dolphins, Anderson has earned the nickname, "the Sticker." In the pros, when a defensive back delivers an especially hard tackle, they say he really "stuck" the ball-carrier. Anderson makes more than his share of those tackles.

Unlike Buoniconti, Anderson came to Miami straight out of college—the University of Colorado. He was with Miami during the dog years when the Dolphins could hardly get out of their own way, much less anybody else's. But he learned.

"For those first years," he said, "football was work. Now it's fun. When you respect the people you play with, when they're good people, and you're on a good team, there's nothing like it."

Dick Anderson grew up playing football. His younger brother, Bob, a running back with the Denver Broncos, provided the perfect companion.

"Every night of the season, when we were growing up, we would be in the yard playing football or playing catch with a football," he said. "We were always competing, either with somebody else or with each other."

As a thirteen-year-old in the eighth grade, Dick

started out in organized football—his team had a coach and regular practices were held after school. But he did not start as a defensive back. In junior high and high school, he was a quarterback. Still later in high school, he was a fullback and a defensive back. It wasn't until he reached college at Colorado that Anderson became a safety. He has been one ever since.

"What I remember most about my football career," he said, "is that at each stop along the way, more of my contemporaries dropped out. From grade school to high school, the field narrowed. From high school to college it narrowed still more, and then it was really cut in that last jump to the pros.

"Some people lost interest. Some did not care to make the sacrifices. Others simply did not have the ability to move on to the next level. The point is, people competed at every level. And they kept on playing as long as they found satisfaction or value. This is important to me. If you don't try something, you'll never know how good you might have been."

Anderson is one of those athletes who can do anything well. He is an excellent skier and a splendid golfer, often breaking par. Bruce Devlin, the pro golfer, once said he thought Anderson could have made a career of being a golf pro had he not chosen football.

On the Dolphins, he teams with Jake Scott to give Miami what most coaches feel are the best defensive safeties in football. Close friends off the field, Scott and Anderson own a ranch together in Colorado.

Anderson, in the undefeated 1972 season, led the Dolphins in fumble recoveries with six, intercepted three passes, made 74 tackles, returned five punts, and punted four times himself.

"He can do anything you ask," Coach Don Shula said.

In his first five full seasons as a Dolphin, Anderson played in 55 of 56 regular-season games. He leads the team in career interceptions, with 24. In 1968, he led the old American Football League in interception returned yardage with 230, including a 96-yard touchdown run. That was the year he shared All-AFC rookie-of-the-year honors with Oakland's George Atkinson.

There they are. Nick Buoniconti and Dick Anderson, All-Pros on the only undefeated championship team in the history of professional football.

Now they're going to tell you how to play their game.

Middle Linebacker

NICK BUONICONTI

YOU DON'T HAVE to be big to enjoy football. Tough, yes. Gutty, yes. Willing to make sacrifices, yes. Size is something not everybody has. But size is relative. I'm 5′11″, 215 pounds, but that isn't big for a middle linebacker in professional football. Dick Butkus of the Chicago Bears weighs 245. Linemen go 250 pounds and up. Even running backs are bigger. Our own Larry Csonka weighs 235 pounds, and if you don't think stopping a 235-pound runner is a tough assignment, then you have another think coming.

The point is, compared to the men I compete against, I'm small. In high school, a person playing my position could weigh 150 or 160 pounds and still be an excellent middle linebacker capable of competing with other players his age.

Heart and the willingness to sacrifice have much more to do with success in football. You have to be willing to practice in the mud and the rain and the heat when your friends are off boating or hanging around a soda fountain. You have to be willing to play when it hurts a little. Every scrape and bruise shouldn't send you whining to mother or the team trainer. You want to play a man's game, then learn to act like a man. Be tougher than the next guy. Not just physically tough, but mentally tough. Be a disciplined person.

I planned to be a middle linebacker when I was ten years old. The first day of practice I was running across the street in borrowed equipment when I slipped on wet pavement. I broke my arm. That put me out for the year. But I came back the next year and won the middle linebacker job from more experienced players. I won because I was quicker, I tackled harder, and I forced myself to be just a little smarter than the competition.

The biggest part of being a middle linebacker is quickness and aggressiveness. That has been my strength—that and brains. A middle linebacker must be smart. He has to be a leader. The other players on defense look to the middle linebacker to

This is the proper stance for a middle linebacker, feet spread evenly and parallel to each other.

lead. He must provide that leadership. When the going gets tough, they will be looking to you. If you don't have leadership qualities, then it will be very, very tough to become a middle linebacker.

Now, how do you play the position?

First, the stance. You should take a parallel stance, meaning your feet should be evenly spread about the width of your shoulders. By keeping your feet parallel and your hands in front of you, you are offering a blocker the minimum target. A stance featuring one foot well in front of the other would offer a blocker an unnecessary target.

The parallel stance also allows you to move easily in any direction. Your weight should be on the balls of your feet. Don't lean forward, but just feel the weight on the balls of your feet. This allows you to shift your weight to meet a blocker or to pursue a runner. Take a flex position. This means your knees should be slightly bent, your body in a crouched position. This puts you in a ready position to move in any direction.

The responsibilities of a middle linebacker defending against the run are to fill holes in front of him as quickly as possible and to pursue rapidly to the outside to take away the "lane" a running back looks for when he wants to cut upfield on an end sweep.

On pass coverage, you must backpedal quickly to your assigned position. By backpedaling, you are able to keep your eyes directly on the quarterback all the way to your area of responsibility. This is important. As you drop in a backpedal, you will be able to see a draw play or delayed handoff. If you turn your back to the play to retreat to your zone, you naturally lose sight of the ball.

Usually it is the middle linebacker's job to call defensive signals. This is important. Everything starts with the middle linebacker calling the defensive alignment in the huddle. His teammates look to him for leadership and effective play-calling is one means of establishing that leadership.

When the going gets tough, it is up to the middle linebacker to make the big play. Many defenses are designed to allow him maximum mobility and maximum freedom. He has to want to hit, to want to make the tackle, to want to be in the thick of the action.

The three best middle linebackers I can think of in professional football are Mike Curtis of Baltimore, Dick Butkus, and Willie Lanier of Kansas City.

Curtis excels because of his great quickness. He can plug holes, cover to the outside, and drop quickly and deeply on pass situations. And he likes to hit people. Butkus is big and strong. He likes to try to tear off a guy's head when he makes a tackle. He intimidates a ball-carrier. He makes people not want to run with the ball. When you can do that, half your battle is won. This separates Butkus from the rest of the linebackers—his ability to deliver the big hit.

Willie Lanier of the Kansas City Chiefs combines the best attributes of Butkus and Curtis. Lanier is a hitter, he's quick, and he's smart. Larry Csonka once said running against Lanier was like running against a grizzly bear, only Lanier was a smart grizzly.

If you want to be a middle linebacker, remember:

1. Establish leadership.
2. Take a proper parallel stance.
3. Plug inside holes and shut off cut-back lanes.
4. Make a quick drop on pass coverage.
5. Be willing to sacrifice.

Outside Linebacker

NICK BUONICONTI

AN OUTSIDE LINEBACKER is a different breed of cat altogether. He has to have a little of the speed of a defensive back. He has to move some size and muscle. He has to have quickness, and he has to have brains.

The speed he needs for covering backs on pass patterns. Almost always, it falls to the outside linebackers in man-to-man coverage to cover the running backs coming out of the backfield and into the pass pattern. So an outside linebacker has to have enough speed to run with an O. J. Simpson or a Mercury Morris or a Jim Kiick.

While he is called on to cover fast backs, he also must protect the outside on end sweeps. To do this he has to fend off blocks by guards and tackles in order to hold his position on the line.

He has to be quick when called on to drop back into zone pass coverage. This means he has to master the backpedal, so important to linebackers and defensive backs.

And he must be smart enough to read his keys quickly. Is it a run or a pass? A sweep or an off-tackle play?

The outside linebacker's principal responsibility is to turn in the end run. Any time you see an end run succeeding, it usually means the outside linebacker has not given what we call "support." Support means he gets up the field, across the line of scrimmage, to take on a pulling guard or a blocking back. The linebacker's job is to turn the run inside so somebody else can make the tackle. If the outside linebacker is knocked out of the play, allowing the running back to get outside, it becomes virtually impossible for the pursuing middle linebacker and defensive tackles to stop the play.

His second responsibility is to take the halfback on man-to-man pass coverage. It is asking a little much of a linebacker to keep up with O. J. Simpson, who runs the 100-yard dash in something like 9.4 with his pads on. So the linebacker has to find an edge. He finds it by jamming.

Jamming is simply giving the back a hit when

he comes out of the backfield into the pass pattern. This has the dual effect of slowing him down and knocking him out of his pass route. Even an instant's delay is enough to cause a pass play to break down. My strong advice, however, is don't miss the back when you go to jam him. If you miss an O. J. Simpson and he gets past you, he's gone for a touchdown pass. When you want to jam, hold your ground. Don't go after your man. Let him come to you. If you move after him, he'll sidestep and be gone. Be patient and set yourself. Give the receiver a good forearm or a good shove, and then run with him. Don't forget this. Jamming will just slow the man up, it won't stop him. You must jam and run.

Outside linebackers have one tremendous advantage over other defensive players. Because of their position on the outside, they can see everything unfold. The play always develops in plain view. They are in the perfect position to deliver big hits on runners.

I'll never forget seeing Roy Winston of the Minnesota Vikings hit Larry Csonka last year. Winston is an outside linebacker. Csonka was out on a pass pattern. Winston was covering him. Csonka turned his back to catch the pass and Winston hit him going full speed. It looked as if Larry snapped

This is the stance for the outside linebacker on the right side. My feet are wide spaced, but the right foot is slightly in front of the left. My hands are up to fend off blockers. My body is turned slightly toward the football.

On the right side, the outside linebacker's stance remains basically the same except that my left foot is forward. My body is again angled toward the football.

in two. He was out four or five plays. A lesser man would have been out for at least the game and maybe several games.

Winston was only doing his job. Your object on defense is to hit a ball-carrier or pass receiver so hard he won't forget it. You want to make him not want to carry the ball again, especially anywhere near where you're going to be.

An outside linebacker's stance differs from a middle linebacker's. On the outside, don't take a parallel stance. One foot should be in front of the other. The right outside linebacker, for instance, should be in a crouch with his left foot forward. His body should be angled so he can look directly into the backfield. The parallel stance isn't necessary for an outside linebacker. He is playing only one side of the field. Unlike the middle linebacker, he doesn't have to be ready to move in either direction. The play is either going to come directly at an outside linebacker or away from him. In any event, it will unfold in plain sight.

An outside linebacker's overall job is to protect his side of the field first. He must protect himself from the people who can block him. A weak-side linebacker—the linebacker away from the tight end—should have his left foot forward and his left forearm up to protect himself. He knows there will be only two people who can block him, the half-back or the pulling guard. So he should be alert for these people.

It is very important for an outside linebacker to use his hands. He must keep blockers away from his body. So he has to get his hands out in front of him to fend off blockers. An effective measure when plugging a hole is to greet blockers with a forearm, trying to straighten them up so the linebacker can establish control.

On pursuit, use your hands. Don't go with a forearm. The important thing in pursuit is speed. A forearm takes too much time. When you're on the move, fend off blockers with your hands. When you want to hold your ground so you can plug a hole, then use your forearm to straighten up a blocker.

The best outside linebackers, I think, are Chris Hanburger of Washington and Andy Russell of Pittsburgh. These guys are underrated, but smart. They know what down it is, the situation, the yardage, where the ball is on the field, how far for a first down, what the quarterback might be likely to try in a certain situation. They know how fast a halfback can run, how deep guards pull on running plays.

These guys have intelligence, toughness,

strength. They are ready for the crackback block or to fill a hole or to cover a pass receiver. They aren't particularly big, but they're quick and they can deliver a solid shot. They never quit. They give 100 per cent all the time. This is what it takes to be an outside linebacker, to be a good football player.

Remember:

1. An outside linebacker's first responsibility is to turn in an end run.

2. When jamming a back, wait for him to come to you.

3. Take a stance that allows you to view the entire field of action.

4. Use your hands to fend off blockers, your forearm to straighten them.

Defensive Ends

NICK BUONICONTI

THE DEFENSIVE END: everybody's hero on defense. He's out there in open view. He's tall, tough, long-armed, maybe even capable of leaping tall buildings at a single bound. Of all the defenders, defensive ends become the best known. Perhaps it is because they so often are rubbing the quarterback's face in the dirt. The champion of "the sack" is the defensive end.

There's Bubba Smith at Baltimore and Bill Stanfill at Miami, Deacon Jones at San Diego and Claude Humphrey at Atlanta. There's Gerry Philbin and Jack Gregory, Jack Youngblood and Carl Eller. Even National Football League folklore is dotted with the names of defensive ends who cast a shadow of terror over the league; guys like Doug Atkins with the Chicago Bears for so many years and Gino Marchetti of the Colts.

Okay, you can be famous as a defensive end. But before that, you have to have the qualities to become one. You need height more than heft, quickness rather than brute strength, and brains to go along with your brawn. And you have to be tough. Don't worry about being noticed. That will come. Who was the first player selected in the NFL's 1973 draft? John Matuszak, the 6′7″, 270-pound defensive end from tiny Tampa University in Florida. Houston plucked him.

What is the defensive end's principal responsibility? I would have to say it is getting to the quarterback, applying strong pressure in a passing situation. That's number one. After that, he must be able to turn an outside play back to the inside. That's two. Third, he must be able to cover to the inside. He's one of the most versatile guys on the field. He must be as quick as a linebacker and almost as strong as a defensive tackle.

Height in his position is more important than weight. This is because his first responsibility is to the passer. When he applies that strong rush, hands held up over his head, he forces the quarterback to throw over him, cutting hard into the accuracy of the pass.

The defensive end lines up slightly outside the shoulder of the offensive tackle, who, 99 times out

This is the basic, three-point stance for defensive ends, tackles, and middle guards.

I am the left defensive end. I'm lined up on the outside shoulder of the offensive tackle. The right defensive end is on the outside shoulder of his offensive tackle.

of 100, has the assignment of blocking the defensive end if the play is coming in that direction. Like that of an outside linebacker, the defensive end's responsibility is to get to the outside quickly. He absolutely cannot afford to get hooked inside by the offensive tackle. That leaves the outside protected by only one man, the linebacker, who, in most cases, will have to cope with two blockers—the pulling guard and a lead back—in the absence of a defensive end.

On the Dolphins, the defensive end has what we call a "two-gap" responsibility. This means he has his outside responsibility, but he also cannot be blown off the line of scrimmage (pushed backward) and then turned to the outside. So he must be able to maintain his position on the line in case he suddenly is called on to close down on a hole that is opening inside of him. This is a difficult assignment, but not complicated. The defensive end must first keep from getting blown out of his position by the tackle's original charge and then must be prepared to rush the passer or protect the outside, as the situation dictates.

Often the defensive end must ward off a double-team block. This block is a combination effort by the offensive tackle coming straight out from his position and by the tight end blocking down from

In a grab-and-shake technique, n
first move as a defensive lineman
to grab the blocker hard by the
shoulders . . .

. . . Then I shake him as hard as I
can, trying to throw him off
balance . . .

. . . After I have the blocker mov
in one direction or the other, I s.
hard with his momentum and m
past him.

the defensive end's outside shoulder. The object is to blow the defensive end off the line of scrimmage and open a hole that can be filled only by the now overworked outside linebacker.

When he is being double-teamed, the defensive end should only try to maintain his position at the line of scrimmage, even if he has to go to his knees to do it. The important thing is not to be taken completely off the line and out of the play. No one expects a man under a double-team to make the tackle, knocking aside two blockers. But coaches do expect him to hold his position.

Now, rushing the passer. How? Rule number one is to get a jump on the ball. The instant it is snapped, the defensive end must be moving. Step one is to get your hands on the defensive tackle. Get your hands in front of you and on the tackle. Control him. By control, I mean you are moving him, he isn't moving you. With your hands, you want to move him either left or right so you can take either an inside path or an outside path to the quarterback. You do not want to try to go straight over the offensive tackle. Usually he is just as big and just as strong as you are.

One way to get around your man is with a head slap. I saw Ernie Ladd use this technique very effectively one year on Billy Neighbors, who was

As a defensive lineman preparing to execute a head slap, I take my regular stance . . .

. . . My first move is to hit the offensive blocker hard on the side of helmet . . .

. . After making contact, I push hard away from my body, at the same time starting to move past the blocker . . .

. . . To complete the maneuver, I move quickly beyond the blocker, continuing all the while to push him away and past me.

then playing tackle for the Dolphins. Ernie caught Billy a terrific shot on the side of his helmet. He knocked Billy right off his feet, stepped past him, and sacked the passer. The trouble with using head slaps is that they are a high-risk maneuver in addition to being tough to learn.

The basics are simple. Plant your opposite foot and give the blocker a hard, swinging shot with your open hand on the side of his helmet. The difficulty is that this takes a great deal of strength and coordination. If you miss the slap, you've had it. Your midsection is left open to the blocker. He'll move you right out. I would not advise it for a young player.

The most important thing for a young player is to watch the ball and get used to moving on the snap. After that, control the blocker with your hands. As you control, you can move outside or inside. Most vital, though, is getting off the ball first. If you let the offensive tackle set up in his pass-block position, chances are you will never overcome his advantage and never get to the passer.

Know the passer you are rushing. If he's a drop-back passer, you can go either inside or outside the blocker depending on which is easier. If he's a roll-out quarterback, never go inside. You will be putting the blocker you just avoided between you and the route of the quarterback. When rushing a roll-out passer, always rush from the outside. He's too tough as a roll-out passer to risk a straight inside rush.

Your best stance at defensive end is a three-point stance, feet spread, body forward on the front two or three cleats of your shoe, one hand down touching the ground lightly. Your back should be parallel to the ground, not slanting to the rear like a dog sitting down. Do not rest your weight on the knuckles of your down hand. When you do that, you only force yourself to push up before moving forward.

Your goal is to move on the snap of the ball as quickly as possible. Your head should be up, looking at the tackle, ball in view out of the corner of your eye.

Remember, as a defensive end you must:
1. Protect to the outside at all costs.
2. Hold your position when double-teamed.
3. Move quickly off the ball.
4. Control the blocker with your hands.
5. Take a three-point, fingertip stance.
6. Keep your head up, watching the tackle in front while keeping the ball in view out of the corner of your eye.

Defensive Tackle

NICK BUONICONTI

I'M A MIDDLE LINEBACKER now, have been one all my professional football life. But that doesn't mean I was always a middle linebacker. In college at Notre Dame, I was a defensive tackle as a sophomore. Buoniconti a defensive tackle? He's too small. Maybe, according to the standards in professional ball. I was a 5'11", 190-pound defensive tackle. And I liked it. I played the best game of my college career at defensive tackle.

It was in 1961. Notre Dame was playing Michigan State early in the season, but already it was billed as the game of the year. We were both 3–0 and both considered contenders for the national championship. They beat us, 17–7, but, as a defensive tackle in a losing cause, I was voted lineman of the week by the wire services. I made 17 un-assisted tackles in that game. It was the highlight of my college career. And remember I was 5′11″, 190 pounds.

I told this little story to illustrate a truth I've never forgotten. I realized the reason I was able to make those 17 tackles was not because of size, but because of quickness. That quickness allowed me to get off the ball and avoid blockers.

One of a defensive tackle's greatest attributes is quickness and strength. These come first. Size, relatively speaking of course, comes next. You have to have some heft to play defensive tackle, but a man in professional football weighing 240 pounds can be a better defensive tackle than a man weighing 280 just because of quickness. The same thing holds true in high school football. A 30-pound weight advantage can be overcome by quickness.

The perfect example is Manny Fernandez, the defensive tackle for the Miami Dolphins. Manny is 6′2″, 240 pounds, very small as tackles go in professional football. Yet he made 16 tackles in the Super Bowl against the Washington Redskins. He made those tackles despite his lack of height, weight, and eyesight. Manny is so nearsighted he can barely make out the number of the offensive guard lined up across from him.

Manny Fernandez depends on speed and quickness to make him one of the best tackles in football. He has good strength, but he relies on speed and quickness. I've seen him chase down fleeing quarterbacks, man on man. In 1972, on the way to beating Buffalo 24–23 in the Orange Bowl, Manny burst into the backfield so quickly that he took the ball right out of the hands of Dennis Shaw, the Bills' quarterback, and ran for a touchdown. Quickness pays big dividends.

Now to the mechanics of defensive tackle.

The primary responsibility is to the inside, the gut-middle, just as the defensive end's primary responsibility is to the outside. The tackle is responsible for blocking up what we call the "zero" hole —that's right over center—and the short trap plays, where there is a fake and a delay before the blocker tries to "trap" the defensive tackle, who is supposed to be lured away from his position.

I think of a defensive tackle almost as another middle linebacker because there are so many different people who can block him. He has to be on the lookout for all of them. He can get hit by the guard immediately in front of him, by a tackle

Here, as a defensive tackle, I am lined up head to head with the offensive guard. My face must be in line with his face.

blocking down on him from his outside shoulder, or by the center from his inside shoulder. He can even get hit by the other guard coming across to block him. So the defensive tackle has to be a little smarter than the average defensive player. He has a lot of decisions to make in a split-second's time.

The defensive tackle, then, must play straight into the guard opposite him. That's one. If the guard pulls, he must look for somebody else blocking him. Is it the center, the tackle, or the other guard? Really, a defensive tackle ought to have eyes on both sides of his head.

The most important thing to remember in a defensive tackle's original charge is not to come up straight. He should shoot out of his three-point stance in a crouched position, low to the ground. If he comes up straight, he's too good a target for a blocker. His stance should be the same as a defensive end's, weight evenly distributed and slightly forward, but not resting on his down hand. He should be ready to spring like a lion out of his stance when the ball is snapped. He wants to get to that offensive guard and control him before the guard has a chance to set up properly. He must always stay lower than the blocker.

Like a defensive end, sometimes a defensive tackle will be double-teamed. He must hold his ground and not be taken out of the play. To cope with a double-team block, a defensive tackle should shift his weight from the offensive guard first trying to block him to the center who is supplying the double-team in an effort to wheel the tackle out of position. Very seldom will a defensive tackle break the double-team. But the important thing to do is hold ground, fall down if necessary, and keep the hole small.

Another important thing to look for is the short trap by the offensive guard. As the guard playing opposite him pulls to the outside, a defensive tackle's inclination is to take a step in that direction. As he takes that one step out and he finds no one is blocking him, his first assignment is to look back quickly to the inside. When he sees the other offensive guard coming to trap him, the defensive tackle must lower his shoulder, shift his weight to his inside foot, and hold his ground against the offensive guard trying to block him. If he holds his ground, he has done his job. It is then up to the middle linebacker to make the tackle.

One of the most common mistakes a young defensive tackle makes is lining up too close to the ball. A defensive tackle should take his three-point stance about a yard off the ball. This way he can see the guard in front of him, the center, and the tackle. On any running play, it is much better to be a yard off rather than right on the nose of the offensive guard. If you can see all three potential blockers, you can see which one is going to try to block you. If you're too close, you can be trapped too easily. Again, Manny Fernandez in the Super Bowl lined up about a yard to a yard-and-a-half off the offensive guard. Because of this, he was always able to see who was trying to block him and prepare for the block.

In a passing situation, it's a little different. You want to be as close to the guard as possible, nose-to-nose. When the ball is snapped, you want to be on the man as quickly as possible in order to control him before he can set up.

Always keep in mind that the defensive tackle is guarding a very vulnerable spot in the middle. He must close that hole. He can't be off chasing rainbows.

In reviewing the defensive tackle position, the points to remember are:

1. Develop quickness.

2. Always hold your position in the vulnerable middle.

3. Make your charge low; never straighten up.

4. In running situations, line up one to one-and-a-half yards off the ball.

5. In passing situations, line up nose-to-nose with the offensive guard.

6. Be wary of the short trap.

Middle Guard

NICK BUONICONTI

YOU RARELY SEE a middle guard in professional football. The sophistication of our offenses and defenses makes the middle guard position unwieldy in pro football because his job is to protect more against the run. The middle guard places four instead of five men on the defensive line. Naturally, as the name implies, he plays directly over the offensive center.

Colleges and high schools and junior leagues often employ middle guards instead of middle linebackers. This is not to say there never are or were middle guards in professional football.

In a playoff game in 1972 between the Washington Redskins and Green Bay Packers, Washington used a middle guard much of the game. Manny

Sistrunk played over center. The Redskins wanted to stop Green Bay's good running game. They did it with the middle guard. Later, in the Super Bowl, there was talk of Washington's using a middle guard against the Dolphins, but the Redskins did not. They couldn't, really. Bob Griese is too good a passing quarterback. Without that extra linebacker whom the middle guard replaces, a good passer can pick apart a defense. Green Bay, which likes to run as much as Miami, didn't have a quarterback who offered a threat like Griese.

Probably the most famous middle guard in history was the late Les Bingaman, a former Dolphin coach. As a player with Detroit, Bingaman was an All-Pro, 300-pound middle guard. Not many teams ran against the Lions when Bing was there.

The best I've seen recently is Rich Glover, the middle guard on Nebraska's great college team. He isn't big—5′10″, 230 pounds—but he's strong and quick. As I've said before, strength and quickness go a long way to make up for lack of size.

As a middle guard, you want to remember the same lessons a defensive tackle learns. Do not, in a running situation, line up nose-to-nose with the center. Back off a yard so you can keep the center and both offensive guards clearly in view. One of

The middle guard lines up directly over the offensive center. Here, I am anticipating an offensive run, so I line up about one yard off the ball.

Now I'm the middle guard planning to rush the passer. I'm lined up so my down hand is almost touching the ball.

these three men, or two on a double-team, will be trying to block the middle guard.

Take a three-point stance, weight on the balls of your feet, fingertips of your down hand touching the ground, back parallel to the ground, head up. Now you're ready to play football.

If the center comes out to block you, he's going to go one of two ways. He'll either come to you straight on, or he'll try to get his head in front of you on the right side or the left side.

If the center comes straight on, the middle guard must first meet the charge with a forearm to the chest of the center in an attempt to straighten up the man. After the center is straightened, then the middle guard can control him with his hands and move either right or left. Do not try to out-guess the center and make a charge to the right or left on your own. If you guess wrong, the center has no trouble taking you out of the play and creating a tremendous gap in the defense.

If the center tries to get his head to one side of your body, you know he will be trying to move you in the opposite direction, using his head as additional leverage. If nis head is on the right, the play will be going to the right. When you see the center moving to the left or the right, it is vitally important to get your two hands on the center and your head outside of his. You control him, then move in for the tackle.

When the center tries to get his head between you and the ball-carrier, we call it a "cut-off block." When you see him doing this, it is important to get your hands on him. Do not in this instance try to straighten him with a forearm. You don't want to use your forearm, because you don't want to become entangled with the center trying to block you. If you do, he'll take you off your feet, and you'll be out of the play. By using your hands and getting your head in front of his head and controlling him, then you'll be able to beat him to the point of the ball, the point of attack. If you can do that, you'll be in position to make the tackle.

Many times a middle guard will be double-teamed. The center will come out, plant his head in your chest, and try to straighten you up. We call this "posting." One of the guards then will block down on you from the side. The important thing when being double-teamed is to do what the defensive ends and defensive tackles do. Hold your position. Plant your feet when the center makes contact. Shift your weight to take the force of the guard's block. If necessary, go to your knees. But hold your position. Don't let them drive you out.

In a passing situation, second and eight or longer

than third and seven, it is a little different. The middle guard must get nose-to-nose with the center. The instant the ball is snapped, get your two hands on the center to control him and move quickly to one side or the other to initiate your pass rush. Quickness here is essential. If you control the offensive center, you can get to the quarterback. If you control him by moving him to the right, then go to the left and vice versa.

Your review steps as a middle guard are:

1. Line up in running situations a yard to a yard-and-a-half off the ball.

2. In passing situations, line up nose-to-nose with the center.

3. Control your blocker with both hands if he tries to take you left or right.

4. Meet the center with a forearm to straighten him on straight-on blocks.

5. On double-teams, hold your ground.

Safeties and Cornerbacks

DICK ANDERSON

As in everything, to learn to play defensive football properly, you must begin at the beginning. The beginning in this case is not running outside and knocking the mailman sideways with a bone-crusher of a tackle. The tackling will come later. First, if you want to be a safety or a cornerback, you have to learn to position yourself in a stance that leaves you comfortable, relaxed, ready, and very important, an unknown quantity to the quarterback readying his attack.

Before we get into the stance, let me tell you what I mean about unknown quantity. At this level of football, all quarterbacks are looking for some key to help in understanding what the defense they face will do when the ball is snapped. Zone? Man-for-man? Double coverage? Single coverage? If the quarterback knows what is going to happen, he can cut a defense to pieces.

So your first job is not giving him any clues. In an exhibition game last year against Green Bay, before we began on our undefeated streak, a rookie safety played most of the way for us. Green Bay's quarterback watched him and soon determined precisely what we were going to do. If our safety was planning to move to his right, he had his right foot back. When he was going to go left, he would have his left foot back. In his own mind, our safety thought he was giving himself a split-second edge in moving in the direction he wanted to go. Maybe so. But he was also telling the quarterback everything he needed to know to beat us, which the Packers did. We didn't find out what we did wrong until after we had watched the game films for one solid week.

A lot of clubs have their defensive backs line up a certain way. Not all are the same. Even individuals differ. Lem Barney of the Lions, for instance, has his own style and there is nobody else quite like him. Jake Scott and I, on the Dolphins, take slightly different stances. But we take the same stance every time. This is important: We take the same stance every time.

The standard stance for defensive backs. Notice that my feet are spread, knees relaxed, body crouched, and head up for good vision.

This stance is almost the same. But notice that my body faces more to the outside, or sideline. This would be more of a cornerback's stance, ready to take the wide receiver down the sideline.

Now then, to the stance. First the position of the feet. There are two ways, both acceptable. The way I stand, and the Dolphins stand, my feet are at 45-degree angles and open toward the quarterback. This provides me with the best view of what the offense is doing, from wide receiver to quarterback. The other position is a closed stance in which your inside foot is slightly forward of your outside (closest to the sideline) foot. Cornerbacks often prefer this stance. It gives them a little better jump covering a wide receiver's short outside pass pattern.

Remember—the most important thing about the position of your feet is to keep the same position every time—zone or man-to-man, whatever coverage. Don't try to cheat a little. Think of it as taking an examination at school. If you cheat, the one person you're going to hurt most in the long run is yourself. Quarterbacks aren't stupid.

All right, your feet are positioned. Now flex your knees slightly. Not a deep knee bend, but a slight crouch. You can't expect to get off the mark quickly if you are standing as stiff and straight as a praying mantis. My college coach would come up behind us and give us a hard shove to see if we had our knees properly flexed. If we didn't, we would be easily pushed out of our tracks. If we did, we could absorb the shock and still be in our ready position, prepared to move equally well in any direction. When your knees are properly flexed, you should feel springy, slightly on the balls of your feet.

Now, relax. You cannot be tense when you are waiting for the play. Tenseness will destroy your concentration. When I first started playing college football and even into pro football, I was not relaxed. My legs were as stiff as concrete pipes. That is one of a veteran's big advantages today. He knows how to relax. A rookie doesn't. Even after four years as a pro, I was tense in our first Super Bowl against Dallas in 1972. They beat us badly, and I was burned my share of the time. The next year, when we beat Washington 14–7, I was a different man. Totally relaxed. Ready, alert, but relaxed. I know it made a difference in my play.

Now that your feet are positioned, your knees are slightly flexed, and you are relaxed, look at the offense. Your stance must yield what I like to call "proper vision." This simply means you can easily see everything you have to see of the offense without swiveling your head like a turkey.

I must be able to see the entire offensive team. As a strong safety, I want to be able to see the tight end in front of me, and the wide receiver out of the corner of my eye. I want to be able to see the quarterback, all the other backs, and the offensive line. This is one reason the position of the feet is so important. This is the reason I prefer the open stance. I can see everything best from this position.

Overall, I want to stress that the important thing is to be comfortable. When you are comfortable and relaxed and your feet are properly positioned, then you know you are prepared. You haven't given the offense any free advantage. It will have to earn what it gets from you.

So remember:

1. Position your feet at 45-degree angles, an open stance facing the offense.

2. Flex your knees.

3. Relax.

4. Maintain good vision of the entire offense.

5. Be comfortable.

Assignments

DICK ANDERSON

THE BASIC DEFENSIVE philosophy of the Miami Dolphins is simple in the extreme: Do your specific job in a particular defense, and *then* react to the ball. Okay, I can see people scratching their heads and saying that any dummy knows he has to react to the *ball:* If there is a tackle to be made, there sure isn't any sense in making it on a man who doesn't have the football. But the important thing is to do your job first. Very important. Complete your assignment first, then go chasing after the ball. No successful defense is a one-man gang. He might look spectacular racing around, making all the tackles. But if one man makes 80 per cent of the tackles, then he is either leaving his job to somebody else, or everybody else is leaving his job to the guy making all the tackles.

This won't work. Your team will lose if you depend on a one-man gang defense. That is why it is so important to do your job first. If you do it and do it right, then your teammates have confidence that they can carry out their assignments without covering a hole that you might have left to gallop off somewhere. The basis of a good defense is every man having confidence that every other man is doing his job.

The reason the Miami Dolphins have been successful is that each member of our defense carries out his own assignment first. The broad responsibilities are not difficult to define. I have outlined some of them before. On the Dolphins, cornerbacks and safeties look for the pass first, then react to a running play. Linebackers must be ready to react either to run or pass. Linemen look for the run first, then go for the pass rush.

Ideally, each member of a defensive unit knows the job of every other member. Sometimes it takes a while, but it pays off. I like to call this knowing the defense. If you know your own job, fine; but nothing can equal that feeling of security you have when you know that somebody else will be supporting you, and you know where he will be and where he will come from. When you understand everyone else's job, you understand that you aren't out there alone.

Mental preparation is important. Before a game, you should know everything possible about your opponents. The Dolphins, for instance, the week of a game, spend an hour and a half in a morning meeting discussing the other team, an hour in the afternoon watching films, and then another two hours on the field implementing what was learned in classroom sessions. Many of us also take home films to watch during the evening. I understand that at the junior high and high school level, this kind of devotion to the game isn't possible. School comes first. But then the game you play is not as complicated as ours. A little study at your level will go a long way.

One thing I have always done, from Optimist League through the pros, is to put myself mentally in situations I think might happen on the field. I work out beforehand in my mind exactly what I should do in a given instance. I like to know whether a team favors run or pass on second down, who the prime receiver is in certain situations, what their tendencies are on short-yardage plays.

I know I've mentioned this before, but I can't stress it too strongly. You must train yourself to react instinctively to a situation. The time to do your thinking is the week of the game, not the day of the game. In a game, if you stop to think, it is going to be too late to carry out your assignment by the time you finally determine what you should do.

So, to review your assignments:

1. Know thoroughly the defenses your team plays.

2. Prepare yourself mentally for the game.

3. React to a situation without having to think it out.

4. Know the assignments of the other members of the defensive unit.

Tackling

DICK ANDERSON

ANYBODY WILL TELL YOU that football is first of all a game of hitting. True enough. And I have to think a defensive player likes to hit people more than an offensive man. Hitting is what defense is all about. You want to knock somebody down, you hit him hard. The essence of the perfect tackle comes from what I call "the explosion" of a tackler into a ball-carrier. This is nothing more than concentrating all of your drive and energy at the point of impact with the ball-carrier. Believe me, runners remember when they have been nailed with a solid shot. Defensive players build their reputations on their ability to hit people hard and cleanly.

Our outside linebacker, Mike Kolen, is a good

example. In college at Auburn his nickname was Captain Crunch. He still has the same name in the pros. He really crunches people. He makes more perfect "explosion" tackles than any other player I can think of. When I first came up to the pros, they called me "the Sticker." When you hit somebody solidly, we like to say that you "stuck" him. Hence, "the Sticker." I like the name. It showed that I was doing my job. Maybe I got a little carried away at times. I became so intent on being the Sticker that I sometimes neglected to wrap my arms around the man I was trying to tackle. I depended on the force of the blow to knock him down. The Sticker got stung a few times when the ball-carrier didn't fall and kept on going for more yardage.

There are a million wrong ways to tackle. You see them all the time. The most common, I would guess, is the arm tackle. Guys who don't care to hit are specialists at the arm tackle. Instead of putting their bodies into the tackle, they duck away and try to snag a runner with an arm. Ridiculous. If you're that gun-shy of tackling, maybe you ought to take up some other sport. For one thing, I've found over the years that the easiest way to get hurt playing football is not to play hard. The guy who gives the toughest lick is the guy who is going to stay healthy. You're delivering the punishment then, not taking it.

There are plenty of different styles of tackling, depending on who is to be tackled. There is one approach for big backs like Larry Csonka, and another for fast backs like O. J. Simpson, and still another for pass receivers. But there is one standard, perfect tackle every defensive player should master. The perfect form tackle devastates the runner and leaves the tackler with that sense of satisfaction in knowing he has done his job with precision.

In the perfect tackle, your head should hit the runner right in the numbers, then you pick him up and drive him back for a loss.

The steps in the perfect tackle are:
1. Head up.
2. Eyes wide open.
3. Neck arched.
4. Knees bent and flexed.
5. Head in the runner's numbers on the front of his jersey.
6. Arms wrapped around the runner.
7. Drive through the man and knock him backwards.

Most important here is keeping your head up

This sequence shows the perfect form tackle. In the first picture I am moving into the ball-carrier. I am crouched, my head is up, pointed at his chest . . .

. . . I make contact. My knees remain flexed. My head is in his numbers. My arms are ready to lock behind the runner . . .

. . . Now I explode into the runner, keeping my head in his chest and locking my arms tightly behind his back. My momentum should carry him backward, with me ending on top as he falls.

and your eyes open. For heaven's sake, keep your eyes open. I've seen so many youngsters squinch their eyes closed at the moment just before impact. If the ball-carrier decides to change direction, the tackler with his eyes closed is standing there out of luck and looking foolish, grabbing at air or a limp leg.

The trouble with the perfect tackle is that you don't get to use it as often as you would like. While you would like to plant a perfect tackle on every runner, the runners are uncooperative. You must, however, make sure to wrap your arms around the runner and hold him. And you must keep your feet during the tackle. The flying tackle is something you read about in story books. Once you leave your feet on a tackle, you have left behind your means of generating power.

Tackling a fast man in the open field, where a defensive back operates, involves more than setting yourself for the perfect tackle. The most important thing here is to get some sort of hold on him. Get a grip on a leg or an arm or a neck, anything to slow him down. Don't dive at a fast man. You're gambling everything on making a sure hit and knocking him down. If you miss that dive, there may not be anyone left between the runner and a touchdown. Try to get an angle on a fast man. By that, I mean take him some way other than head-on. This gives him less room to maneuver, takes away a lot of his moves. If you're coming at him at an angle, about the best a runner can hope for is to use his raw speed to outrun you. Also try to force a fast man to the inside where you have help from your teammates. If he gets outside and past you, there isn't anybody else.

Big men like to punish tacklers. And they can do it. Size is to their advantage. The most punishing big man I know is our own Larry Csonka. He weighs 240 pounds. His legs are like tree trunks. When he runs head-on into a defensive back, the small defender is getting all the worst of it. Csonka knows this. I know a lot of defensive backs hate to see him coming through under full power. Another back like Larry is Wayne Patrick of Buffalo. He weighs 254 pounds, and he will punish you.

The best way to get at a big man is from the side. He can't use all that muscle and force on you then. You can hang on until help comes. Naturally, big men know this. They try to force you to take them head-on. When you have to do it this way, my advice is to junk the perfect form tackle. The weight and speed are so much in favor of the big man that he can trample right over a defensive back. Instead, go low for the shins or the knees.

In tackling a big man from the side, come in low, ready to knock him off his feet . . .

After making contact, keep your feet, driving into the legs of the runner . . .

Try not to leave your feet until the runner is downed and the play is dead.

Try to knock him off his feet right away. You aren't going to punish him, anyway. What you want to do is go low and knock him down. If you get him going sideways, remember to put your head in front of him and drive through, keeping your feet. It is important on any tackle from the side to put your head in front of the runner and drive through. Don't get your head behind him. Then your momentum is driving you away from the runner rather than into him.

Tackling a receiver is something else entirely. Of course, if he has already caught the ball and is legging it downfield, you get him any way you can, remembering to keep your head in front if possible and to wrap your arms around him. There is something else that defensive backs call "the moment of truth" for a receiver. This is when you hit him at the precise moment the pass reaches him. You hit him hard. If your timing is right, he'll remember it. He'll hear footsteps the next time he's out for a pass. Maybe that time he'll be worried more about getting hit than catching the ball.

After a receiver has caught the ball, the split second after, it is important to hit him full force. Often you will make contact just as the receiver turns upfield. He won't have control of the ball as well as he should. A good hit there can force a

After the receiver has caught the pass, a good defensive back should try to strip him of the ball and cause a fumble. Here, I move in on the receiver the instant he catches the ball . . .

After making contact, I put my arms through his and try to force his two arms out from his body, away from the ball . . .

fumble and turn a big gainer for the offense into a big play for the defense.

I recall one of the best shots I ever delivered was in 1969. I was playing free safety then. We weren't the Dolphins we are now. We were in last place, playing Oakland, which was in first. It was muddy and raining, and the score was tied. Daryl Lamonica sent Warren Wells on a pattern over the middle. Just as the ball got to Wells, I hit him with everything I had. Perfect hit. Perfect timing. I really got him. But he didn't drop the ball. No fumble. No recovery. Oakland kept the ball and drove on to a field goal by George Blanda that beat us 20–17. Sometimes even your best effort doesn't return the dividend you would like.

The point I want to make here is that, whenever possible, you want to make a tackle as close to the perfect form tackle as you can. Do it the right way. Nine times out of ten, you'll be happy with the result.

When tackling, remember:

1. Head up, eyes open.
2. Keep your head in front of the man.
3. Hit him in the numbers.
4. Wrap your arms around the runner and lock them.
5. Keep your legs pumping and driving.

Pass Coverage for Defensive Backs

DICK ANDERSON

THERE IS ONE cardinal rule in pass coverage. It applies before anything else. Don't let a receiver get behind you. Don't let him get between you and the goal line. If he does, and the pass is there, it's a touchdown. No matter what else you do, do not let the receiver get behind you.

Just from a point of pride, this can be devastating. (So can the resulting touchdown.) Nothing is quite so open to the fans' view as deep pass coverage. It's just you and the receiver. If he gets free behind you, 80,000 people are sitting up there in judgment, and there isn't any place to hide. There isn't any sharing blame or responsibility. You're the goat. I don't think there is a safety alive who hasn't gotten beaten for a touchdown. They all

68

know that awful feeling in the pit of the stomach when they're chasing somebody who has just caught a touchdown pass over their head.

A defensive back always must think of the pass first and the run second. If you start thinking run first, you're going to be beaten a lot. Your primary job is to stop passes.

There are three basic types of pass coverage: man-for-man, blitz, and zone. Every team employs all three at least part of the time. The Dolphins are known primarily as a zone team, but we blitz and we use man-for-man. Everybody uses man-for-man near their own goal. You have to. You can't afford to give up those short passes that a zone will yield.

The man-for-man coverage is just what the name implies. Each defensive back has a specific man to cover, and he covers that one man throughout the play. The two cornerbacks take the split end and the flanker, the two wide receivers. The strong safety takes the tight end. The free safety usually helps the cornerback on his side of the field. Incidentally, the strong safety isn't named for his physical strength. It is just a designation given because the strong safety lines up on the same side of the field as the tight end, which in football is called the strong side of the offense. Usually the free safety is the faster of the two safeties. His

This is my basic position with regard to the receiver in pass coverage. I am crouched and relaxed.

Now the receiver is moving at me. I am already starting to backpedal, keeping three yards between me and the receiver.

The receiver cuts to the right. I watch him carefully and move the instant he does.

When he goes to the left, I follow the same procedure, watching the receiver and moving when he does.

job is a little more wide-ranging than the strong safety's.

Man-for-man coverage is the toughest type of coverage. You defend against just one man. He changes from week to week, so your task is never exactly the same. Every receiver presents a different problem. Usually, tight ends are not as fast as wide receivers. This is a break for the strong safety, but there is always the exception. Rich Caster of the Jets is a big tight end who can run the 100 in 9.5 seconds. So he presents a real problem. Cornerbacks have even greater problems. I don't know how I would cover our own Paul Warfield. I don't think it is possible for one man to cover him. He's fast, has great moves, and has great hands. The only way to cover him is with two defenders.

In pass coverage, it is vital to be able to backpedal, which is nothing more than running backwards. When the play starts and the man you are covering moves at you, you should be backpedaling, slightly crouched, keeping a cushion of two to three yards between you and the receiver. The cushion gives you reaction time. Do not turn to run until you have to. Naturally, you can't backpedal forever, but the idea is to keep it up as long as possible. By backpedaling, you accomplish two things—you keep your receiver in front of you, in full view, and you have full vision of the quarterback.

Blitz coverage is similar to man-to-man coverage. You line up five to seven yards off your man, waiting for the play to begin. But you keep in mind that the blitz will force the quarterback to throw more quickly. You must be prepared to defend against the pass a split second after the ball is snapped.

Many teams use bump-and-run coverage in blitz situations. Some of them also use bump-and-run as a steady diet. Oakland does. Oakland, in fact, popularized the bump-and-run. Buffalo also uses it a lot. There isn't anything complicated about bump-and-run.

In this defense, the defensive back lines up nose to nose with the receiver. The cornerback lines up either head-on or a touch to the inside of the wide receiver. The job of the cornerback is to bump him as he comes off the line, knock him off stride. The wide receiver can go three ways—straight ahead, trying to bowl over the defender, or inside or outside. This is where study comes in handy. If you know in which direction your man is likely to go in a given situation, then you have an advantage. You can anticipate his move.

In this type of coverage, the defensive back must

Interference: Defenders cannot grab and hold a receiver.

Interference: Defenders cannot "clothesline" unsuspecting receivers headed out for a pass.

Interference: Once a receiver is past a defender, the defender cannot push him.

Interference: A defender cannot intentionally block a receiver's view of the ball.

assume a solid stance because you know you are going to have contact. Your arms and hands should be up and chest height because you have to push the receiver off balance on his first step. The real term probably should be push-and-run. The bump-and-run is risky when you have receivers like Paul Warfield and Howard Twilley—quick receivers. Because you're so close to the receiver, it only takes one quick step to get past you. This shoving and pushing keeps going in the bump-and-run even while the receiver is running downfield. You can push the receiver off course until the ball is in the air. After that, pushing constitutes pass interference. Neither can you push the man once he is beyond you. This also is pass interference.

So the three times bump-and-run is used are blitz coverage, goal line coverage, and, in a few cases, as the basic coverage by teams who favor it.

Zone coverage rapidly is becoming the predominant defense in pro football. The Dolphins use it most of the time. Our success probably has had a great deal to do with the growing popularity of the zone. A zone defense, remember, consists of 11 people who have an exact job to do in every instance. There is no free-lancing. The front four—the linemen—always will be rushing. That leaves seven men for the zone—three linebackers and four deep backs. On the Dolphins, we have two types of zone—four short and three deep and five short and two deep.

I can't stress enough that the zone defense will not work unless each man does his job. In man-for-man or bump-and-run, you can make an individual mistake and recover. In zone coverage, you cannot.

In our zone, we will have the three linebackers in short zones about eight yards deep, covering from the line of scrimmage back 10 yards or so. The two cornerbacks will be in the deep outside zones, which means the territory from behind the linebackers to the goal line. The free safety will be in the middle, sort of the centerfielder. And the strong safety will move up to the outside zone on the strong side, the tight end's side. There are many variations dictated by what the offense does. But what you want to remember is to get to your zone immediately, and set up and protect your area, reacting to what the quarterback does. Deep people don't want to let the receiver get behind them. Short people in the zone want to keep the receivers and the ball in front of them.

Finally, when the pass is thrown, sprint immediately to the ball. Converge on the ball. Important now, short men in the zone want to keep backpedaling, keeping the ball and receivers in front of them as the play develops, ready to move up and make the tackle if the pass is dumped short to the fullback or halfback. Deep men must never let a receiver get behind them. If you are in the short zone, try to bump the receivers as they come past you. This is important. Throwing them off their routes can upset the timing.

Remember in your pass coverages:

1. Never let a receiver get between you and the goal line.

2. In man-for-man coverage, maintain your backpedal as long as possible.

3. In blitz coverage, play the receiver tightly.

4. In bump-and-run, push the receiver off balance and stay with him. Do not push when he has passed you or after the ball is thrown.

5. In zone coverage, go immediately to your area of responsibility, then react to the ball.

Pass Coverage for Linebackers

NICK BUONICONTI

THE PASS COVERAGE responsibilities for the middle linebacker and the outside linebackers are different, but not so different as to make them totally dissimilar. The one thing all of us have to remember is that we are not as fast as defensive backs. We must move quickly, anticipate well, and use our strength to work on pass receivers before they can build a full head of steam and get behind us.

In a passing situation, the middle linebacker is in his parallel stance, facing the line. The two outside linebackers are in their crouch stance, either right or left leg forward, forearm resting on a knee, ready to take on the blocker.

In a zone defense, the most important thing to

remember is to make a proper backpedal into your area of responsibility. By proper, I mean the backpedal you learned in drills. Keep your weight forward on the balls of your feet when moving backwards. It may sound funny, but it is the correct way. Otherwise, with your weight on your heels, you tend to build too much momentum. You end up tumbling over on your rear end. Keep your weight forward when backpedaling. Keep your arms close to your body.

In your backpedal, do not turn your head, do not turn your body to the side. Never lose sight of the quarterback. Keep your eyes on him. Drop back quickly to your area of responsibility, which, for the middle linebacker, is about 12 yards deep.

Outside linebackers going straight back use the same procedure. But if they are going to the sideline to take an out pattern away from a receiver, the linebacker must shuffle to the outside. Do not turn and run. Do not cross your legs one over the other. Outside linebackers must not turn. Although it will get you to the sideline faster, it also causes you to lose sight of the quarterback. While your back is turned he could have called a draw play or a screen pass. In either case, a man with his back turned cannot react to the ball. Don't turn and run. You don't cross your legs for the obvious reason. Sooner or later, in your excitement, you're going to get tangled up and trip over your own feet.

A shuffle to the sidelines keeps everything in front of you. The play can be clearly seen. If the quarterback has called a draw or a screen, you won't be embarrassed.

In man-for-man coverage for outside linebackers, do not try to backpedal more than five or six yards. If it looks as if the man you are covering is going downfield, then turn and run full speed right with him. The classic play is to try to isolate a fast back on a bigger, slower linebacker and throw to that back. This is why the linebacker must always be prepared to match a back stride for stride on man-to-man coverage.

The best way to slow down a receiver is to hold your ground at first. The receiver must come out of the backfield and circle around his offensive tackle. When he comes at you, control him with your hands. Give him a shove in front of you. Keep him in front of you as long as possible. You cannot shove a receiver once he is past you. That's pass interference. Jam him with your hands in front of you. This knocks him off stride. Then you can run with him.

However, your initial four or five yards of backpedaling is important. Do not turn and run immediately with a receiver on man-to-man coverage. This throws you out of control. If a receiver breaks to the outside quickly, a linebacker can't recover in time to cover him.

It's most important to backpedal as fast as possible. The faster a linebacker reaches his area of responsibility and sets up, under control, the more time he has to watch the quarterback and to prepare himself to move right or left. A slow drop gives the quarterback time to throw before a linebacker is ready to defend. Interceptions and knockdowns result because linebackers have made rapid drops and are able to react to the ball as soon as it is thrown.

On pass coverage:

1. Make a proper backpedal.

2. Move quickly to your area of responsibility.

3. Never lose sight of the quarterback. Never turn your back to reach your area of zone responsibility.

4. Jam receivers before they can get into their pattern.

5. In man-to-man coverage, turn and run with the receiver after backpedaling the first four or five yards.

Reading Keys for Defensive Backs

DICK ANDERSON

KEY IS PROBABLY the most confusing word you could throw at a youngster learning how to play football. Everybody talks about reading this key and reading that key, and nobody bothers to explain what a key is. A key in football is not unlike a key to the front door. They both unlock something; they both let you inside. The key to the door opens the house. The key to an offensive play tells you what it is and where you must go to stop it. For a defensive back, a key always is an offensive player, a specific player. What he does first determines what you do. So you watch for that primary, or first, key. What he does tells you what you must do.

Before explaining primary keys and secondary

keys, let me tell you what reading keys properly did for the Dolphins this past season when we won the Super Bowl. Our defense, the "No-Name Defense," is comprised of 11 people who work as a unit, doing our specific jobs to make our effort a success. Were we successful? I would say so. The Dolphins last season had the leading defense against scoring, against rushing, and in total yards yielded. I have to give credit for that to Bill Arnsparger, our defensive coach. We're successful because of his brilliance. He can communicate with us. He gets us to do our exact job.

Now there are three basic types of defense—man-for-man coverage, zone coverage, and blitz coverage. You notice there is nothing there about run coverage. A defensive back's first job is to defend against the pass. Only when he is certain there will be no pass does he move up to lend support in stopping the run. Reading keys will be important here. Your keys tell you to stay back for pass or come up for run.

No matter what defense the Dolphins are in or what offensive play is being run, I have a definite job. My first responsibility is to get that job done. After I have done that job, then and only then do I react to where the football is.

In a man-for-man defense, my primary key is

always the halfback. If I were defending against the Dolphins, the halfback would be Mercury Morris or Jim Kiick. Larry Csonka is the fullback. Sometimes defenders call the halfback the "weak" back. All keys are not the same for all coaches or all defenses. It will do no good to explain to you what I do in each of the defensive situations a weak back's move could force. But his first move dictates my first move. That's why he is called my primary key. In every situation there is a primary key. As you grow more experienced, you must look for keys and use them to your advantage.

In every defense I have my exact job to do. What it is depends on my primary key. After I read that key, I react immediately. Reaction is important. A split second literally is the difference between success and failure in stopping a play. I read that first key, and I move. If I have to think instead of reacting instinctively, I'm in trouble. When that primary key moves, I must know what my job is.

In a zone defense, my key remains, in most cases, the weak back. A zone, however, is a little easier to play, in that I have a specific area to cover, and no matter what the key my first responsibility remains this specific and predetermined area of coverage. In blitz coverage, my assignment changes slightly. Since one of our number in the defensive backfield is now rushing the passer, I have a specific person to cover.

In blitz coverage, a strong safety's key almost always comes from the person he is assigned to cover. Strong safeties 99 per cent of the time draw the tight end. If he blocks down, then I must anticipate a run and act accordingly. If he does not block, then I must first assume it is a pass and he is the man I must cover. In a blitz, the weak safety normally will cover the weak back coming out on his side. The two cornerbacks will cover the wide receivers.

Once the play has started and your primary key has told you in which direction to start, you look for your secondary key. Most of the time, this involves picking up a different member of the offensive team. In a man-for-man defense, my secondary key again is the tight end. What he does tells me run or pass. Secondary keys tell you run or pass.

In a zone defense, your secondary key again tells you what to do, although your assignment here is not to concentrate on an individual. If your secondary key blocks, then you should leave your zone to support the defense against the run. If he comes out into the pattern, then you must drop back to cover your area of responsibility.

After I have read my primary key (direction of

play) and my initial secondary key (run or pass), I look for still other secondary keys. The pulling guard, for instance, tells me the type of run. All of this, of course, happens with incredible speed. It takes experience to recognize keys and react instinctively. But begin now to look for keys, training yourself to follow them quickly.

In summary:

1. Define your keys (weak back, tight end, pulling guard).

2. Read your primary key for direction.

3. Read your secondary key for run or pass.

4. React instantly.

Reading Keys for Linebackers and Linemen

NICK BUONICONTI

R E A D I N G   K E Y S   I S   A N important part of defensive football. A key is nothing more than the first indication of where an offensive play is going. This indication is called a key because it unlocks the secret of the play. Each defensive position relies on different keys to unlock the same secret. The positions I'll deal with are middle linebacker, strong-side linebacker, weak-side linebacker, and defensive ends and tackles.

MIDDLE LINEBACKER

This is my position. I remember when I first came into professional football with the then Boston Patriots. In that first training camp, all I keyed were backs. I would look at the backs, find out who had the ball, and go for that man. But I soon found out there were too many counterplays and cross-bucks. I was getting fooled more often than I was guessing right. I was reading the wrong keys.

The Patriots' defensive coach, Marion Campbell, asked me who I was keying. I told him. He said no wonder I was getting fooled. He told me to key "the Triangle." The Triangle is the center and two guards. He said if the center tries to take me straight back, the play is coming straight ahead. If he tries to take me to the left or the right, then the play is going in the opposite direction. The films proved he was right.

Then he told me to watch the guards. If the center blocked left and the guards pulled to the right, I wasn't fooled. I knew the play was going in the direction the guards pulled, and I went with them. Another time I saw a center block left and the guard come straight at me. I knew the play was coming at me so I stepped up, controlled the blocking guard, and plugged the hole.

The Triangle is the key for the middle linebacker. Every time, the members of the Triangle will tell the middle linebacker where the play is going. It doesn't matter what the backs do to confuse you. They can fake and cross and counter all they like, but the direction of the blocking tells the story. So the first thing a middle linebacker must do is read the Triangle.

STRONG-SIDE LINEBACKER

The strong-side linebacker gets his name because he plays opposite the strong side of the offensive line, the side with the tight end. The tight end, then, is the strong-side linebacker's first key because he is most often assigned to block this linebacker.

His secondary keys are the back closest to him, normally the fullback and the offensive guard.

The tight end does one of three things. He tries to block straight on the strong-side linebacker. In this case, the linebacker must meet him with a fore-arm, trying to straighten him up, and control him. The tight end might try to "log" the linebacker to the inside. If so, the linebacker must use both hands to control the tight end, keeping him away from his body and holding him at the line of scrimmage. The linebacker then must try to get his head outside the tight end's. If the tight end blocks down and is assisted by the offensive guard on a pulling double-team, the linebacker must immediately read that the play is going inside of him. His job then is to close down the hole to take away the ball-carrier's inside running room. Finally, the tight end may release to the outside and go downfield as in a pass pattern. We call this "influencing" the linebacker. As soon as the linebacker steps back to cover the tight end, the lead blocking back will try to block the linebacker to the inside, giving the ball carrier a clear path to the outside.

WEAK-SIDE LINEBACKER

His keys are the offensive tackle to his side, the guard, and the running back nearest him. Naturally, there is no tight end. The split end or wide receiver is on the weak-side linebacker's side of the field.

On a sweep to the weak side, the back will try to block the linebacker to the inside or to cut him down so that the pulling guard is left free to turn downfield and block on a cornerback. If the play is going to be an off-tackle run, the near back or the offensive tackle or both will try to take the linebacker to the outside.

The weak-side linebacker always must be on the alert for the "crackback" block. This block is delivered by the wide receiver positioned far outside the linebacker. The first warning that a crackback block is coming will be the lead back or the tackle or the pulling guard passing up the linebacker to block someone else.

The linebacker must always guard against a crackback block. Roy Jefferson of Washington hit Chuck Howley of Dallas so effectively with a crackback block from the blind side that Howley suffered torn knee ligaments and was sidelined for the year. When a linebacker suspects a crackback or hears one of his teammates shout the crackback warning, he should immediately look to the outside, position himself, and bring his body under control to absorb the force of the block.

DEFENSIVE END

On the tight end or strong side, the defensive end must key first off of the offensive tackle in front of him. Next he must key on the tight end, and last, the running back on his side. If the tackle comes straight at him, he must assume the play is coming his way and suspect that the tackle will be getting help from the tight end on a double-team. If the tackle blocks down on the defensive tackle, the defensive end must immediately look for the running back to be blocking him to the inside.

The defensive end on the other side keys off the offensive tackle and the near back on his side. The warning signals are the same as the other end's.

DEFENSIVE TACKLE

His keys are the guard immediately in front of him, the offensive tackle, and the center. The defensive tackle must be aware that all three men can block him. The direction of their blocks is the key to the direction of the play. In the defensive tackle's limited area of responsibility, it isn't hard to figure that if he's being blocked to the inside the play is going outside, and if the center and guard are trying to take him outside, the runner is going inside.

So remember these points.

Middle linebackers:

1. Read the Triangle—both guards and the center.

2. Do not read the running backs.

Strong-side linebacker:

1. Read the tight end first, then the running back and the pulling guard.

2. Control the tight end at the line of scrimmage.

Weak-side linebacker:

1. Read the offensive tackle, guard, and near back.

2. Guard always against the crackback block.

Defensive ends:

1. Read first the offensive tackles, the tight end on the strong side, and then the near back.

2. Protect to the outside.

Defensive tackles:

1. Read the guard first, then the tackle and center.

2. Move to the point of the ball, which always is the opposite of the direction in which the blocker is trying to move you.

Meeting the Run

DICK ANDERSON

THERE IS A DANGER in meeting the run too early. I've touched on it lightly in previous chapters. Now I'd like to give an example. Remember, I have been saying all along that a defensive back must first think pass and then run. Never commit yourself to a running play before you are sure it is not a pass.

In the third game of the last season, we played Minnesota in Minnesota. The Vikings had a good running game, and they relied heavily on it. In the second quarter, they had a third and short situation. Fran Tarkenton, their quarterback, had shown a preference to run on third and short. We knew this. So he called the perfect play. He faked a run. We swallowed the bait and came up fast

95

from our defensive back positions. He threw a 50-yard touchdown pass over our heads.

That didn't happen to us again all year. The point is, we were suckered by thinking run first instead of second. What Tarkenton called was the most difficult play for a defensive back to read. He called a "play-action" pass. This is simply a pass thrown after a running play has been faked. The thing is designed to freeze defensive backs and linebackers for a split second, making them believe it is a run. A split second is all a wide receiver needs to be long gone behind you.

In meeting the run, you must first read your keys. This takes experience, I know. But you must work at it. When the run starts, the safety or cornerback must immediately begin to read his keys. In general, the first key is the halfback. Where is he going? The second key is the flanker or tight end. (Cornerbacks read flankers. The safety reads the tight end). Is he blocking or is he out for a pass? The third key is the pulling guard. Is he pulling, or is he staying at home to pass block? After you have read these keys, then locate the ball. It sounds like a long process, but it isn't. It shouldn't take more than an instant to read all the keys and find the ball. That's what I mean when I say practice and experience are important. You must train yourself to take in all the keys instinctively.

A defensive back has more than one job in meeting the run. Often a defensive back's job is to turn in the play. We call this "support" on the Dolphins. The two most common types of support are safety support and linebacker support. In either case, the safety or linebacker comes up to the outside and turns the play inside, forcing the ball-carrier to cut upfield and into the paths of your oncoming middle linebacker or offside linebacker. The primary job of the support man is never to let the play get outside of him.

The most feared man on an end sweep, from the cornerback's or the safety's point of view, is the pulling guard. He usually outweighs a defensive back by 50 pounds. The best move is to reach the pulling guard before he turns upfield. In that case my momentum, even though he is bigger and stronger, can knock him off his feet. What I never want to do is let just one man block me. I want to force them to use at least two blockers on me, and even then I want to make the tackle. The one thing Coach Don Shula keeps stressing is not to let one man block us.

The best pulling guard in football, thank good-

This sequence shows a blocker coming at me from the side. In the first picture, I lower my arm and shoulder to take the initial shock. After the first contact, I keep my feet and push him away and behind. Still pushing at the blocker, I step around and then move up for the tackle.

Here the blocker is coming at me head-on. With both hands, I take the initial shock. Keeping him at arms' distance and pushing away, I slide to the side away from his thrust. Clear, I look for the ball-carrier.

ness, is Larry Little. He works for us, the Dolphins. They say you can see fear in a cornerback's eyes when he sees Larry coming at him. I don't know if that's true, but it would not take much to convince me. Little weighs 265 pounds, and he is as fast as Larry Csonka. If you have to meet a man like Little head-on, a man bigger than you and stronger than you, your best chance is to go in low, try to knock him off his feet and possibly into the ball-carrier. Create a pileup. If this is impossible, plant yourself as solidly as you can and meet the guard with a forearm, trying to stay on your feet.

When meeting the run, you always have to be aware of the crackback block. This is usually thrown by a wide receiver who is on your outside. He comes back toward the flow and hits you from your blind side. Sometimes this kind of block can be dangerous. An unwary safety or cornerback can come out of a crackback block with a knee injury, because that kind of block almost always catches a defensive back from the side. The best way to avoid a crackback block is simply to keep alert. You must avoid that blocker coming from your blind side.

If you are the first man to meet a play and the ball-carrier has blockers in front of him, your job is to strip the interference while trying to get to the runner. By this I mean sometimes you have to sacrifice yourself to eliminate the blockers, opening the way for a teammate to make the tackle. Stripping the interference takes guts. I think the best example of this kind of guts is guys on the kickoff team whose assignment is to break up the blocking wedge in front of a ball-carrier. Watch them sometimes, throwing themselves at those big blockers.

To review meeting the run, remember these points:

1. Never commit yourself before you are sure the play is not a pass.

2. Read your keys.

3. Provide support to the outside.

4. Never let one man block you.

Techniques of Linemen and Linebackers

NICK BUONICONTI

EACH LINEMAN and linebacker has his own technique. Usually, however, all techniques are nothing more than variations of a standard approach to getting a job done. The head slap is a defensive lineman's technique. The safety blitz is a specialty of the free safety. Looping is practiced by linemen. A standard blitz is put on by a linebacker. The grab-and-shake is a lineman's specialty. I would like to deal with the most widely used techniques one by one, emphasizing that what works for one person does not necessarily work for another.

It should be remembered, though, that the best thing for a young player to do is develop his own technique, refine it in practice, and stick with it. It is much better to do one thing well than five things poorly.

THE HEAD SLAP

This is the most famous technique for a lineman, perhaps because it is so effective when properly executed. Basically, all the head slap entails is slapping the offensive lineman on the side of the head as hard as possible and then quickly moving in the opposite direction to get around the blocker.

The best I ever saw at the head slap were Deacon Jones and Ernie Ladd. Both were big and both were agile. Jones made his reputation using that technique. Ladd was tremendously strong and a terror in the old American Football League.

As I said, the head slap is easy to learn, but hard to execute. And the risks are high. If you attempt a head slap and miss, you are left off balance. Your midsection is wide open to the blocker. He'll easily take you out of the play. I do not recommend the head slap for young players.

THE GRAB-AND-SHAKE

This is my idea of the ideal technique for young

players. Pros, too, for that matter. The idea is to come off the ball very quickly. Move the split second the ball is snapped. Grab the offensive lineman by the shoulder pads and shake him as hard as possible. When you get movement on him to one side or the other, give him a terrific shove in that direction. Then move in the opposite direction.

You want to grab the offensive lineman before he can set up. And you have to shake hard, as hard as you can. A light dance won't do it. I can't recommend this technique strongly enough. It's safe because you do not leave yourself open to the blocker. It's effective if done quickly and with force. And it is not difficult to perfect. The main requirement is quickness, as opposed to the head slap's demands on brute strength.

THE HEAD BUTT

This is a shock technique. As a defensive lineman, you ram your helmet right under the blocker's chin. Do this as hard as you can. This throws the blocker off balance. Usually it drives him back a step, and he has difficulty getting his arms up into blocking position. Once he is set back, make your move to one side or the other.

LOOPING

This is strictly a quickness maneuver. The object is not to make contact with the blocker. A defensive lineman planning to loop is depending on his speed to reach the quarterback. The loop cannot be used as a regular tactic. Basically, looping calls for a quick step to the outside shoulder of the blocker before he can make contact with you. As the step is being taken, you should come across with your outside arm to shove the blocker away from and behind you. This is all one motion—the quick step to the side and the powerful shove with the outside arm. Even though you are planning a loop, you must still line up straight over the blocker. Don't try to cheat to the outside. The blocker will be wise to you.

One great disadvantage of looping is that it can be employed only in passing situations. If you guess wrong and loop on a run to the inside or on a draw play, you will be hopelessly out of position to make the tackle.

BLITZING FOR LINEBACKERS

What makes or breaks a blitz, which is the sudden rush of a linebacker into the enemy's backfield in an attempt to get to the quarterback, is surprise. Everything depends on the offense not being set for a blitz. If it is, it is no problem for an experienced team to pick up the blitzer and block him out of the play. If this happens, the defensive position vacated by the blitzer is vulnerable to attack by passing.

When you blitz, do not reveal it. Never edge closer. Never change your stance. Never do anything out of the ordinary before the ball is snapped. An experienced quarterback will spot it.

On a blitz, remain in your normal position. Try to anticipate the count. If the quarterback falls into a rut—calling all his plays on the second or third snap count—you can pick this up during the game. Then you can anticipate the count and be on the move a split second before the ball is snapped.

Never blitz on your own. You are not a free-lance blitzer. It is part of a prearranged pattern. If I go on the blitz, another member of the defense is assigned to take my pass coverage. Nothing is done on your own. For instance, if I'm blitzing over the outside shoulder of my defensive tackle, he will be stepping down toward the middle. In essence, he will be taking over my duties in the middle while I'll be taking over his to the outside.

Sometimes a fake blitz is as good as a genuine

blitz. This is when you move in close as if you were going to blitz, make false starts, but move back to your regular position at the snap of the ball. This can confuse a quarterback, particularly when you fake a blitz four or five times in a row and then go on the sixth.

THE SAFETY BLITZ

The greatest practitioner of the safety blitz was Larry Wilson of the St. Louis Cardinals. Some say he invented the safety blitz, but I doubt it. Once, in a game against the New York Giants, Wilson blitzed four times and got to the quarterback all four, which is almost unheard of.

The free safety, the one on the opposite side of the field from the tight end, is the blitzing safety.

On a safety blitz, the linebackers do not take part in the rush. They have specific pass coverage assignments. The two outside linebackers must cover the two backs coming out of the backfield and into the pass pattern. The middle linebacker, meanwhile, tries to draw the block off the center, thereby opening a lane in the middle for the blitzing safety.

The free safety lines up seven or eight yards deep, his normal position. He tries to anticipate the count so he is moving at full speed toward the hole before the ball is snapped. Ideally, he should be within a yard of the center at the moment of the snap. Sometimes the free safety will fake a blitz just as the middle linebacker fakes. He's trying to force the quarterback to call an audible, that is change signals at the line, and go for a pass into the area he believes will be vacated by the blitzing safety. A safety blitz usually is combatted by a short pass over the middle. On the Dolphins, we feel if we can convince the quarterback to read blitz and throw that short pass into our basic zone defense, we have a good chance to intercept.

These are your technique review points:

1. Head slaps are high-risk maneuvers.

2. Grab-and-shake is the most effective.

3. In the head butt and the grab-and-shake, quickness is the key.

4. Loop only on passing downs.

5. Blitz with caution and surprise.

Interceptions

DICK ANDERSON

T H E   N U M B E R   O N E   job of the defender is to stop the offense as quickly as possible. The best way to do this is to take away the football. Very simple. No football, no offense. As a defensive back, your best opportunity to take away the ball is going to come through an interception. Which is okay with me. That's about the only chance I get to get my hands on the ball and do something with it. Who among us defensive backs hasn't dreamed of being in a crucial game, losing with only minutes remaining, and intercepting a pass and returning it 100 yards for a touchdown? I never have gotten 100 yards out of an interception return, but I did take one back 96 yards for a touchdown against Boston when I was a rookie.

I'll never forget the feeling of elation I had when I did that.

Of course, the Dolphins were losing then. I doubt if anybody remembers that interception except me and the guy who threw it. My personal high point came in the 1971 American Conference Championship game against Baltimore. We had them down 7–0 when I intercepted a pass and took it 62 yards for a touchdown that put the game out of reach. We went on to win 21–0 and earn our way into the Super Bowl aginst Dallas. But the play people remember in that game was the interception. Not so much the physical act of catching the ball, but the remarkable blocking that took place during my run. That run was replayed on Monday night television and every other highlight show I know of.

Curtis Johnson, our cornerback, deflected the ball back to me. Then the blocking started. Seven blocks. Jake Scott and Mike Kolen knocked the first two Colts off their feet as I started down the right sideline. I cut back. Doug Swift and Tim Foley made two great blocks. Then I cut back again and Bob Heinz and Bill Stanfill, through tremendous blocks, put me into the end zone. I think it stands as the perfect example of what unselfish teamwork can produce. It also shows how you can really sting a team with an interception at a crucial time. That one did everything possible—took the ball away from the Colts, gave us a touchdown, and gave them a terrific psychological blow.

When a ball is thrown, from the time it leaves the quarterback's hand until it gets to the receiver, it's just as much mine as it is the receiver's. In the air, the ball is a free ball. I can go up for it just as strong and just as tough as the receiver. If I outfight him for the ball, then it's mine. I earned it.

Teaching someone how to go up for a ball or whether to knock it away or go for an interception is a difficult thing. Mastering the knack is like riding a bike. The only way to learn it is to do it. And after you know how, nobody can take it away from you. Intercepting passes is a matter of experience.

In going for an interception, the defender should always keep in mind that he must try to catch the ball at its highest point. By this I mean the highest point above the intended receiver's head. The reasoning is basic. If you get the ball at the highest point it can possibly be caught, then you go there ahead of the receiver, and it is your ball. A good drill for a defensive back when working on interceptions is to align himself with the quarterback at midfield. When the quarterback drops back to pass, the defensive back backpedals rapidly. The

In each of these pictures, I am intercepting a pass in a different position. But one thing remains constant. I am always catching the ball at the highest possible point, the key to making interceptions.

quarterback throws the ball either right or left, and high. The defensive back then moves in that direction, leaps as high as he can, and tries to catch the ball at its highest point. Almost all professional, college, and high school teams use this same drill.

In man-for-man coverage, remember that you are covering the man first. Don't let him get behind you while you decide to go for an interception. Stay between your man and the goal line. Zone coverage is slightly different. In a zone defense you must get to a specific point on the field, then react to the ball. As soon as the ball is thrown, you can go for it.

Interference is always a risk. It's a tough call for officials. Only a fine line separates a legitimate play and interference. The key to the call in the official's eyes is whether the defensive back went for the ball or went for the man trying to catch it. If a defender hits his man first and then goes for the ball, interference is sure to be called. If the two go up together and the defender bumps the receiver, there is a 50-50 chance that interference will be called. If the two are running downfield and the receiver is bumped while the ball is in the air, interference will be called. If a receiver gets behind a defensive back and the defensive back pushes him, it is interference. Once a man is behind you, you cannot push him.

This thing goes both ways. The receiver can interfere with the defender. You have just as much right to it as he does. Once in Los Angeles I was covering Lance Rentzel of the Rams. On a deep pattern, I was in perfect position to make an interception. Lance pushed me, then went up and made a spectacular catch at our five-yard line. It would have put the Rams in position to score the winning touchdown. But the official knew what he was doing. He threw a flag on Lance and called offensive interference. All the Rams got was a 15-yard penalty. We went on to win.

In your review of interceptions, remember:

1. When the ball is in the air, it belongs to anybody.

2. Go for the interception when the ball is at its highest point.

3. In man-for-man coverage, don't go for the ball at the expense of letting the receiver get behind you.

4. Don't interfere with the receiver's right to the ball.

Fumbles

DICK ANDERSON

GOOD THINGS HAPPEN to people in the right spot at the right time. It was against San Diego this year, the Dolphins' fifth game of the season, the one in which Bob Griese broke his leg. John Hadl, the San Diego quarterback, had just completed a handoff to Mike Garrett, who was coming around end. For some reason, Garrett couldn't quite find the handle. The ball popped up out of his hands just as I was coming in to make the tackle. There it was right in front of me. I grabbed it out of the air and ran 35 yards for a touchdown. This came at a time when the game was close and could still go either way. It seemed to deflate San Diego. One minute they were moving toward our goal, and the next I had recovered a fumble and turned it into a touchdown. It's a double shock for the offense. It loses the ball and six points.

Fumbles will kill an offense, which I guess is why they are the delight of the defense. The last two years with the Dolphins I've led the team in fumble recoveries, four in 1971 and six in 1972. I don't know exactly why. Recovering fumbles entails a lot of luck. Or does it? You'll never recover one if you're not alert and if you're not where the ball is. That's one reason why it is so important to converge on the ball. You never know what will happen. The only thing of which you can be dead sure is that if you aren't there, you'll never recover a fumble.

Another crucial recovery I had last year was against the New York Jets. They were winning 17–7 when Joe Namath handed off to Emerson Boozer. Just as Boozer was hit, the ball popped out of his hands, took one bounce, and I was right there to fall on it for a recovery. We took that recovery in for a touchdown and went on to win a close one, 28–24.

I mention those two particular recoveries for a good reason. One I grabbed in the air and ran in for a touchdown. The other I fell on for a recovery at the point of the fumble. When do you go for the run? When do you go for the safe recovery?

First of all, I know there are different rules regarding advancing recovered fumbles. In college, you can't advance a fumble. The ball is automatically down where it is recovered. In high school, you can pick up a fumble and run with it, just as you can in professional football. Different junior leagues also have different rules.

However, I try to pick up the ball and run with it when I'm more or less in an open field and nobody is around to knock me off the ball or off stride. In a crowd, I go for the ball and protect it with my body. There is too much risk in trying to pick a fumble out of a crowd of 250-pound men. Chances are you'll get socked so hard that you'll fumble the recovery you just made.

How do you go for a fumble? There's a right way and a wrong way. A proper recovery is more than just throwing yourself at the ball, covering it with your stomach. You don't have any fingers on your stomach. You can't get a grip on a ball with your rib cage.

When the ball is on the ground and you're going for it, keep your eye on the ball all the time. Just as if you were catching a pass. Keep your eye on the ball. That way you're not going to grab grass instead of football. Grab the ball first with your

Grab the ball in both hands . . .

To recover a fumble, move with legs flexed and hands outstretched to pick up the football, much the same way a shortstop fields a grounder.

Without breaking stride, bring the ball up to the protection of your midsection.

Tuck the ball under your arm and run. You're on offense now.

hands, and then go on down over it with your body, pulling the ball into the midsection and curling your body around it. Make a kind of protective shell out of yourself. This keeps the ball from being jarred loose while it offers you the best possible protection from people trying to knock you off the fumble.

If you're going to pick it up and run with it, again go for the ball with your hands. Think of yourself as a shortshop in baseball going for a hot grounder. Get your hands out in front of you, bend your knees, spread your fingers wide, and make sure you go for the ball in one smooth, continuous motion.

A smooth motion is important. You want to get the ball and bring it in close to you before you are hit by somebody else. The defense works hard to force turnovers. If you have a chance at a fumble recovery, don't blow the chance by overeagerness or slipshod technique. Get your hands on a fumble first, then your body. I've seen too many players, even at the professional level, who see a loose ball and simply throw themselves at it. The ball hits their helmet or shoulderpads or knee and bounds away into somebody else's arms. Being first on a fumble is not enough. What is important is to be there first and to make the recovery.

If you choose to run with the recovered fumble, remember that you are now a running back. Tuck the ball safely under your arm and near your body. Don't you fumble. I can't think of anything more disheartening than recovering a fumble or making an interception and then losing the ball right back on a fumble of your own.

It hurts two ways. You lose the ball you fought to get. And the offense has a first down off the recovery of your fumble.

The basics, then, of recovering a fumble are:

1. Be around the ball.

2. Know in advance whether to run with the fumble or fall on it.

3. Grab the ball with your hands first, always.

4. Curl your body into a protective shell around the ball.

Agility Drills

DICK ANDERSON

THE BEST OF US never walked on a football field and established himself as a player without first putting in hundreds of long hours of practice. There is no sense painting it any other way. Much of practice is drudgery. It's hard work. It's repetitious. Sometimes it gets boring. But nobody ever became an accomplished player without working over and over again on the basics. That isn't just in football, either. Figure skaters, for instance, practice six or eight hours a day, much of it devoted to precise routines that are the basics of their sport —the school figures.

In football, I think agility drills are something like practicing school figures. These drills school your body in what you must do to play your position. I do them for a half-hour every day at practice. There are different drills for different positions. I know what demands my position makes of me, so all of my drills are designed to help a defensive back.

On the Miami Dolphins, we pay close attention to agility drills each summer during our training camp. No matter how experienced a veteran you are, Coach Don Shula has you doing the drills until he knows you can do them in your sleep. Later on, during the season, the good players continue with the drills before and after the regular practice session.

Agility is nothing more than the ability to move well, to be loose and free and well-coordinated. The drills are to train your body to respond to the demands of your position.

The best drill, and the most important one for a defensive back, is running backwards. Remember in an earlier chapter we talked about coverage. Your first move as a defensive back is almost always backing up, especially on pass coverage. You see the receiver running at you, and you must run backwards at top speed, keeping him in front of you and three or four feet away.

This requires practice on your part. If you don't think so, go out in the yard with a friend. Have him

This is the proper form for the backpedal drill.

When *backpedaling, keep your body loose and crouched, weight forward.* **Run** *on the balls of your feet.*

run as fast as he can forward, and you race him running backwards. You'll see the difference soon enough.

These are the drills I want you to work on:

1. Running backwards: Take a comfortable stance, the one you would always take during a regular game. There are two ways to move. You can slide your feet or pick them up in a definite running motion. You run backwards with your weight forward. Your upper body and your head should be forward while your feet take you backward. Your body should be in a semi-crouch. Otherwise, all of your weight is moving back. Should you want to stop your backward movement and go with a receiver, you must have your weight forward.

I usually run backwards for 100 yards, turn around and run backwards another 100 yards, and repeat this until I feel I just can't do another 100 yards. Then I do one more. This builds strength and endurance as well as polishing your form.

2. Changing directions: This is a good buddy drill, teaching you to go with the receiver when he makes his cut. Have a friend run at you at top speed as the receiver while you run backwards.

When he makes his sharp cut left or right, make a cross-over step, planting your inside foot and coming across your body with your outside foot. If your first step with the receiver's cut is made with your inside foot, he'll be gone. That's your pivot foot. It produces power. Take the long step with the crossover and then push with your pivot foot.

3. *Breaking to right or left:* Again, you start the drill by running backwards. Your buddy is the quarterback. While you run backwards, he signals quickly and at short intervals with the ball, indicating by a motion of the ball whether you should cut sharp left or right, or left or right at a 45-degree angle. This drill is doubly helpful in that you are once again practicing running backwards, and at the same time you are responding to the football. When he gives you the direction, break out of your backpedal and sprint left or right, just as if a receiver had made his cut. Your buddy can also throw passes off this drill, giving you a chance to practice interceptions at the same time.

4. *Coming straight forward:* Another buddy drill. Be running backwards, watching your partner holding a football. When he slaps the ball, immediately plant your feet and run forward. Sounds

Here I am practicing the crossover step, legs scissoring one over the other.

easy, but don't neglect this drill. As long as I've been playing, this one still is the toughest for me. Its value is in training you to come forward to meet the run after you have been in a backpedal.

5. *The crossover step:* Run forward swinging your legs high back and forth across your body. Pick your legs up as high as you can and swing them with authority. It's sort of like moving forward and changing direction at the same time. Another good drill is to cross over going sideways, moving laterally with first one leg and then the other in front of your body. This drill gives you balance and strength.

All of these drills are much easier to do, and much more fun, when you can do them with at least one other person. Make contests out of the drills. See who can run backwards the fastest. See who can intercept the most passes without dropping the ball. See who has to quit first for a rest.

Let me stress once more the importance of drills. Each one embodies the basic moves you must make as a defensive back during a game. The more second nature these moves become, the better able you are to do your job. Nobody ever became proficient at this game without working. Agility drills are work. But they must be done.

Punting

DICK ANDERSON

THE PUNT IS A pretty darn good defensive weapon. A good punter can do two things with one punt. He can get his team out of a hole and put the other team into one. On the Dolphins, Coach Don Shula evaluates our punting game just as he would our passing or running attack. He compares how well we did with how well the opposition did. For instance, if our total yards returning punts is greater than theirs, because our punter hung the ball so well they couldn't get return yardage, then we have an edge in the punting game. That's what Shula looks for, an edge here and an edge there. Add up all the edges and you have the winning margin.

One of the beauties of learning to punt is that it's

fun. The first thing anybody wants to do with a football is kick it. There is no drudgery involved. There's something satisfying about hearing your foot meet the ball just right and watching the ball spiral away and arc far downfield.

I punted most of the time for Colorado when I was in college. With the Dolphins, I'm the number two punter behind Larry Seiple. He's much better, but sometimes I have to fill in. He was hurt this year against the Jets—a knee injury. I was called on to punt once in that game. I hit one for 37 yards that was downed on the Jets' nine. It turned out to be a big punt, pinning them deep in their own territory. We won by only four points, 28–24. The other time I punted was against the New York Giants in our 13th game. I averaged only about 36 yards a punt, but I was satisfied. It was muddy and windy, but I didn't have any blocked.

I usually devote at least some part of two practice days a week to punting. I enjoy the practice. But even while it's fun, I still work on each punt exactly as if I were in a game. I take the same steps, use the same follow-through. I don't clown around. The game should be the application of what you have learned and perfected in practice. Shoddy practice habits will show up during a game when it counts. Take your practice seriously. Concentrate on what you are doing. Don't try to punt a ball backwards over your head. You'll never be called on to do it in a game.

The stance for receiving a punt varies slightly from player to player. It is not unlike your stance as a defensive back, one foot slightly in front of the other, body crouched ready to receive the center snap.

Most punters use either a two-step or a three-step approach. A right-footed kicker using a three-step stance will have his left foot forward in his stance. When he receives the snap from center, he will take a step with his left foot, then his right, then his left and kick the ball. A two-step punter will start with his right foot forward and take a step with his right, then his left and kick the ball.

When lining up to catch the snap from center, a punter in professional football is 15 yards deep. This is too deep, of course, for junior league centers and perhaps too deep for high school centers. Use judgment, but stay back a safe distance so the punt is not blocked.

When waiting for the ball, I keep my two little fingers touching to be sure that my hands are forming a cup. The worst thing a punter can do is drop the snap from center. That creates all sorts of trouble.

Ready to punt, I have the ball waist high, feet almost together.

In the three-step punt, my first step is with my left foot.

Ball still waist high, I take my second step.

As I take the third step, I begin to release the ball.

After contact, a complete follow-through is essential.

Just as if you were receiving a pass or making an interception, keep your eye on the ball until you have caught it securely in your hands. Only then do you start into your steps approaching the kick.

The drop of the ball is extremely important. Picture dropping the ball with the point down a little bit and angled in a little bit. Drop it with two hands. Drop it from no higher than waist high. I've seen players who didn't know better start their drops from above their heads. This is ridiculous. The farther the ball must fall to meet your foot, the more chance there is to make a poor drop.

Your foot should be arched, your toe pointed. The ball should hit the arch of your foot as it swings through. Follow through. This imparts the spiral to the ball, and this is most important. Just as in passing, a punter must look for a spiral. This gives the punt distance by allowing it to cut through the air. Floaters or end-over-end punts will not achieve nearly the distance of a spiral.

It is important to follow the same routine punt after punt. Always make your drop from the same height. Always hold the ball the same way. Always have your foot arched. Always follow through. Your goal is to make the mechanics of a punt second nature, just like combing your hair. A good punter probably could go through his steps, meet the ball, and produce an acceptable effort with his eyes closed.

Remember these rules when punting:

1. Keep a relaxed stance, one foot in front of the other.

2. Watch the ball into your hands.

3. Make your drop from waist high.

4. Keep your toe pointed and foot arched.

5. Follow through.

Returning Punts

DICK ANDERSON

RETURNING PUNTS is a high-risk business. Drop one and the other team has a first down, usually deep in your territory. That is the worst damage. Of course, there is your own ego to be considered. You usually are back there all by yourself in full view of 80,000 people and who knows how many more watching on television. There isn't any place to hide after dropping a punt. The thing to do, then, is to make sure you catch it.

Most teams have a defensive back returning punts. On the Dolphins, Jake Scott is our number one returner, the deep man. I'm the short man, about 12 yards in front of Jake. It's my job to field short punts or, if Jake takes the ball, to throw the first block. I guess defensive backs make good punt returners because by nature they are reckless and accustomed to pressure. Most of us have good hands.

Punting is really a defensive maneuver by the offensive team. They're in trouble. They can't move. So they go to the punt. It makes defenders out of the offense and offenders out of the defense. And it gives the defense a chance to score. Not a great chance, but a chance.

A properly executed punt return, as in any other properly executed play, is designed to go all the way. Coach Don Shula works hard on punt returns. His philosophy is that the Dolphins are going to have an edge in every part of the game, and that includes specialty teams. A lot of people have said our specialty teams are the best in football. It isn't any accident. Shula works us hard. Every man has a specific job, and every man had better be prepared to do it.

The mechanics of every punt return are basically the same even though the flow of the return may be either left or right. The punt returner's job is to know the direction of the play. The linemen are to hold up the punting team coming downfield to make the tackle. Then they curl back downfield and set up what we call "the blocking wall" near the sidelines.

In fielding a punt, my hands are high, ready to take the ball above my head.

I look the ball into my hands, never taking my eyes off it . . .

I bring the ball in toward my midsection . . .

Finally, I tuck it tightly under my arm and become a ball-carrier.

Ideally, the returner fields the ball cleanly, loops back slightly, and heads toward the sideline where he cuts upfield, hopefully behind a man-made wall formed by his blockers. That's the ideal return. Unhappily for a punt returner, that sort of return doesn't happen often.

On the Dolphins, we use two men deep. Jake is the primary return man. I'm the short man. Our first goal, and the goal of any player returning punts, is to field the ball cleanly before it hits the ground. Always catch the ball. A cardinal sin in returning punts is to let the ball bounce.

A bouncing ball creates two hazards. First, you can lose up to 20 yards on a punt by letting it hit and roll. Second, and perhaps more important, it can bounce into one of your teammates. If it touches one of your men, the ball can be recovered by the kicking team.

Always be sure of your catch. That's the first thing. Don't worry about where you're going to run or how far it is for a touchdown or how close to you is the nearest defender. Catch the ball at all costs. Jake Scott in three years with the Dolphins has dropped only one punt, and that because he was hit just as he went to catch the ball.

How do you catch a punt? Okay, first practice, practice, and more practice. My personal technique, and the one I recommend, is this. I put my hands high, waiting for the ball. The fingers are spread. I have the tips of my little fingers touching so I know I have made a kind of basket. Watching the ball all the way I first make contact with it high, just over my head and in front of my face. In one motion I cradle the ball and bring it down into my midsection and tuck it away. Keep your elbows in tight to your body. Think of your arms as a basket. But most of all, DO NOT TAKE YOUR EYE OFF THE BALL FOR AN INSTANT.

After you catch the ball, then worry about running with it.

When do you fair-catch? When do you go for the return? A matter of judgment again. Always fair-catch in a crowd or when a defender is close enough to give you a good shot just as the ball reaches you. The fair-catch signal is one hand held high over your head. Hold it high. Don't be hesitant. You want to tell the official and those guys coming down under the kick that this is a fair catch. After a fair catch, you cannot advance the ball.

Go for the return when you have some open space, even if it is enough for only a five- or 10-yard return. The two men back on punts should help each other. Since the man fielding the punt

The fair-catch signal is one hand raised overhead in this manner.

should have his eye glued to the ball, his partner should be yelling fair catch or not at him. Sometimes, though, in the heat of the game and with the noise from the stands, you can't hear any advice. At times like this, instinct and judgment and experience are going to pay off.

The general rule in football is not to fair-catch any punt inside your own 10-yard line. Let the ball hit. Most likely it will roll into the end zone and you'll get the ball on your 20. Fair-catching inside the 10 can only cost you yardage.

The short man, particularly, should be sure-handed. It will be his job to field short punts. Usually they are high and usually you are surrounded by the punt coverage. Dropping a punt in this situation almost always will result in losing possession. In a crowd, fair-catch. Don't pay any attention to the defenders. They can't hit you no matter what on a fair catch and, under any circumstances, not until after you have made the catch. You have the right to an unimpeded catch.

If the short man does not catch the ball, his responsibility is to block the first man downfield. This is important. That one block might be enough to spring loose the returner on a long gain.

Remember, then, on punt returns:

1. Know the direction of return.

2. Know whether to fair-catch.

3. Hold your hands high, palms open, little fingers touching, elbows in close.

4. Keep your eye on the ball all the way into your midsection.

5. Don't let the punt bounce. Catch everything on the fly.